MW00354615

*Art washes away from the soul the dust of everyday life.*

—PABLO PICASSO

**CATS BRING COLOR TO OUR LIVES** with their playful antics and particular style. We love them for their independent nature, their graceful movements, their athletic prowess, and their quiet, calming presence. In this tribute to fantastic felines, honor the cat companion in your house by unleashing your inner artist and bringing out the many dimensions and details of these unique drawings. Experiment and have fun; use realistic tones or a rainbow of hues—it's all up to you! Paired with inspiring quotes about the wisdom of cats, we hope this book allows you to unplug, unwind, and discover talents you didn't realize you had.

# Tips to Make Your Cats Look Fur-Real

**COLORING IS SUPPOSED TO BE A STRESS-FREE,** no-worries activity. There really is no right or wrong way to do it. But if you'd like to take it to another level, here are some step-by-step instructions and helpful tips that can take your pages from meow to wow, as you can see in the example on the following pages.

STEP 1 Pick your palette. For this example, we chose gold and brown tones for the cat. If using pencils you can get different variations of the same color by applying more or less pressure with the colored pencil. Begin with light pressure and then use a heavier hand if you want a more intense shade, or add more of the same color on top to get the layered effect that will add interest to your picture.

STEP 2 Think about the light source in your picture; the shading of the fur depends not only on the color of the cat but the way that the light is hitting the cat's fur, and from which angle. Light and shadows add depth to the drawing.

STEP 3 As you color, make certain that your strokes go in the same direction that the fur grows on a cat. It's easy to see this in most of the illustrations.

STEP 4 Start with the lightest colors, deciding where those areas will be, and do them all first. Then continue coloring—in the direction the fur grows—with the rest of the colors in your palette. Keep in mind that it is easier to start light and go darker than to try to make an area lighter.

STEP 5 Finish off the fur with the darkest color, keeping in mind your light source.

STEP 6 Step back and look at the picture from a distance and you will see if you need to add any more details.

STEP 7 Color in the eyes and nose to complete the cat.

**BLENDING COLORS**—By blending several colors together, you can create a three-dimensional shading effect. For example, if you want to color a leaf green, use the color wheel on the next page to choose several shades of green as well as some colors next to the green (yellows and blues). Try to envision where the light would be falling on your image. Wherever the light would fall on the leaf is where you will place your lightest colors (the lighter greens and yellow). Wherever the shadow would fall is where you would place your darker colors (the darker green and a bit of blue). By overlapping the colors and blending them, you will create a realistic effect. It helps to practice on a piece of scrap paper first, and to work slowly to see if you are creating the effect you wish before you complete a large area.

**COLORING THE DETAILS**—You'll notice that many designs are made up of unique doodled designs. You can color each individual element on its own in a separate color, or you can fill in one larger group of shapes in one color.

## A Note from the Illustrator

**I HAVE LOVED DRAWING** and all things artistic for as long as I can remember. I am privileged to illustrate *Inkspirations for Cat Lovers,* and I hope you find as much pleasure coloring the pieces as I did creating them. Use your imagination when you are working on a page; don't be afraid to add your own twists. Some drawings have blank space for you to explore your artistry by adding doodles, interesting textures, or bold colors. We've provided some sample colored images to show you what is possible, and also given you helpful hints and tips. Look at your cats for ideas about realistic hues and shading, find pictures on the Internet, or go in a completely different direction not found in nature. Remember, coloring is only as limited as your imagination!

*—Robyn Henoch*

ROBYN HENOCH *is an artist and illustrator in Boca Raton, Florida. An avid animal lover, gardener, crafter, and all-around DIYer, she's been rescuing kittens and cats since she was a toddler, giving them a loving home. After her beloved cat Foos died at age 22, and Lil' Sugar—a kitten her rescue cat found and rescued—at 19, Robyn saved an abandoned bird who now shares her home. For obvious reasons, she's cat-less for now but brings to life the memories of her many feline friends in this book.*

# Coloring Tips & Tools

**TIP:** Add a piece of scrap paper under each page you're working on to make sure that the ink doesn't bleed through the page.

**COLORED PENCILS:** great for shading or blending colors together, both of which add interest and depth to any design.

**GEL PENS AND MARKERS:** good for adding bold, defined bursts of color.

**CRAYONS:** surprisingly versatile when filling in large spaces.

# Choose Your Colors

**PRIMARY COLORS**
The primary colors—red, yellow, and blue—are denoted by a "P" on the outside of the color wheel. Primary colors cannot be created by mixing any other colors.

**SECONDARY COLORS**
The secondary colors—green, orange, and purple—are shown by an "S" on the color wheel. These are formed by mixing the primary colors.

**TERTIARY COLORS**
Yellow-orange, red-orange, red-purple, blue-purple, blue-green, and yellow-green make up the tertiary colors, which are noted with a "T" on the outside of the wheel. These colors are formed by mixing a primary color with a secondary color.

The colors on the top half of the wheel are considered the warmer colors whereas the bottom hues are the cooler ones. Colors that fall opposite of one another on the wheel are complementary, and the ones that fall next to each other are analogous. You can use both complementary and analogous colors to make a gorgeous piece of art—the possibilities are as endless as your imagination.

# Harmony How-Tos

**JUST AS IN LIFE, BALANCE IS THE KEY** to creating harmony in any relationship—even when coloring. You can find a rainbow of inspiration all around you—in the patterns of plants, animals, flowers, sunsets, and even the morning sky.

## A nature-inspired color scheme with analogous colors

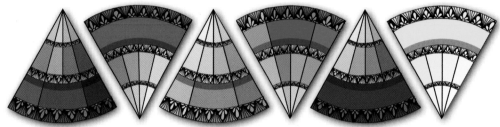

**ANALOGOUS COLORS** are any three colors that are side by side on a 12-part color wheel, such as yellow-green, yellow, and yellow-orange or teal blue, blue, and indigo.

## A nature-inspired color scheme with complementary colors

**COMPLEMENTARY COLORS** are any two colors that are directly opposite each other, such as yellow and purple or orange and blue.

Use the following colored pages as your inspiration. Happy coloring!

Marker art by Robyn Henoch.

Marker art by Robyn Henoch.

Marker art by Robyn Henoch.

Marker art by Parker Lindsay.

Marker art by Parker Lindsay.

Marker art by Leah Honarbakhsh.

Crayon and marker art by Marina Koustas.

Marker art by Robyn Henoch.

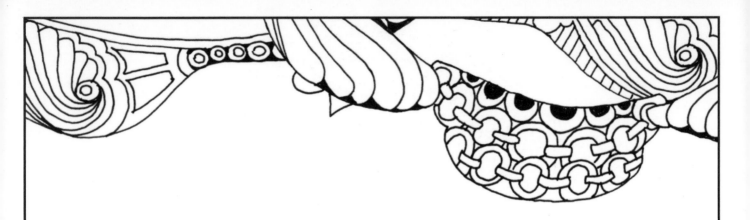

The way to get on with a cat

is to treat it as an equal—or even better,

as the superior it knows itself to be.

—ELIZABETH PETERS,
*THE SNAKE, THE CROCODILE AND THE DOG*

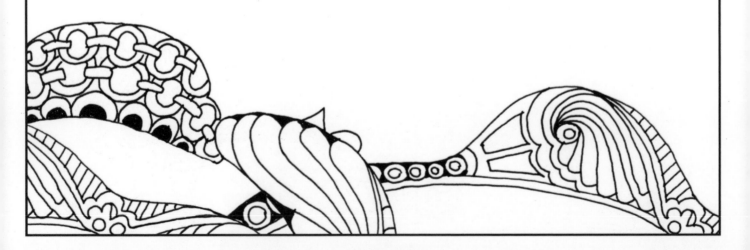

If there is one spot of sun spilling onto the floor,

a cat will find it and soak it up.

—J.A. MCINTOSH

Cats are connoisseurs of comfort.

—JAMES HERRIOT

Kittens are angels with whiskers.

—ALEXIS FLORA HOPE

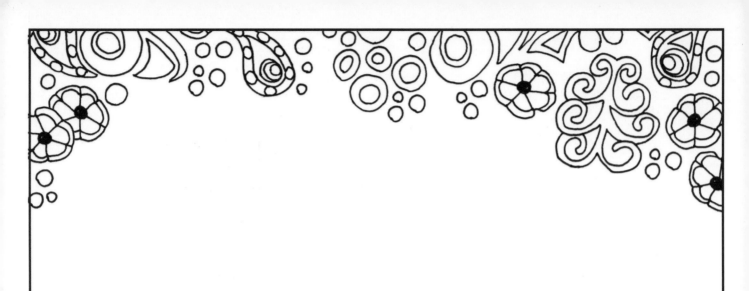

There are no ordinary cats.

—COLETTE

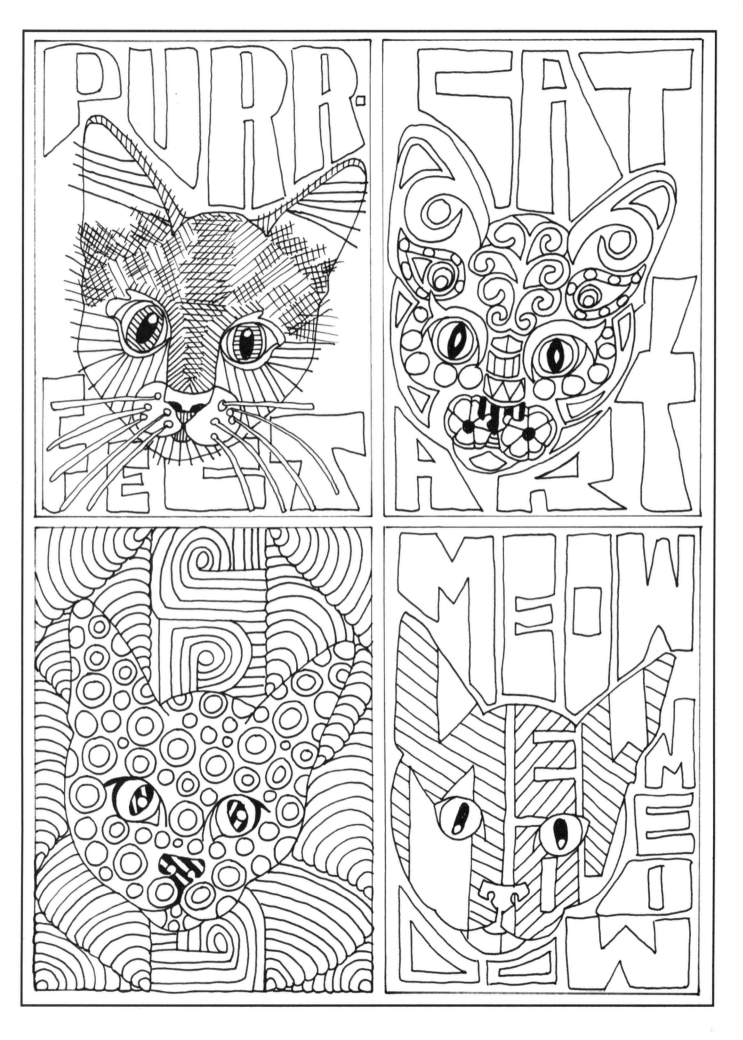

"Meow" means "woof" in cat.

—GEORGE CARLIN

Sometimes the smallest things take up

the most room in your heart.

—A.A. MILNE

There is no need for a piece of sculpture

in a home that has a cat.

—WESLEY BATES

Cats are like music—it's foolish to try
to explain their worth to those who
don't appreciate them.

—AUTHOR UNKNOWN

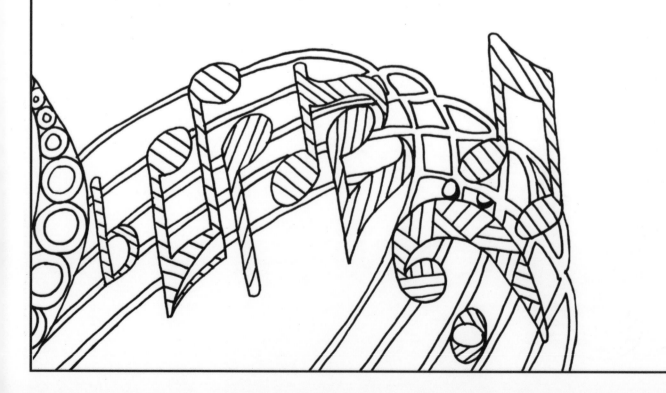

A black cat crossing your path signifies

that the animal is going somewhere.

—GROUCHO MARX

The greatest gift of life is friendship,

and I have received it.

—HUBERT H. HUMPHREY

What greater gift than the love of a cat.

—CHARLES DICKENS

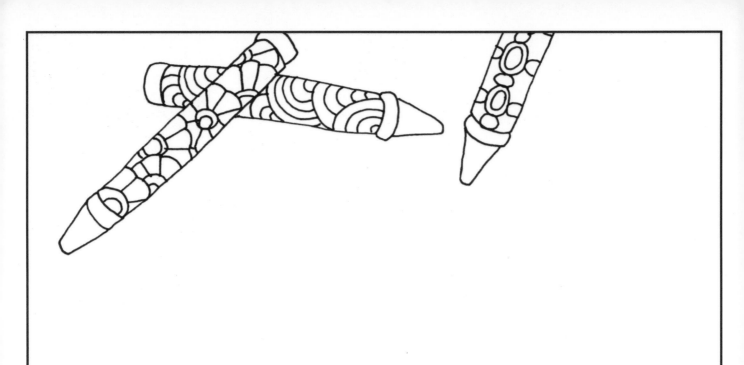

The smallest feline is a masterpiece.

—LEONARDO DA VINCI

A cat can purr its way out of anything.

—DONNA MCCROHAN

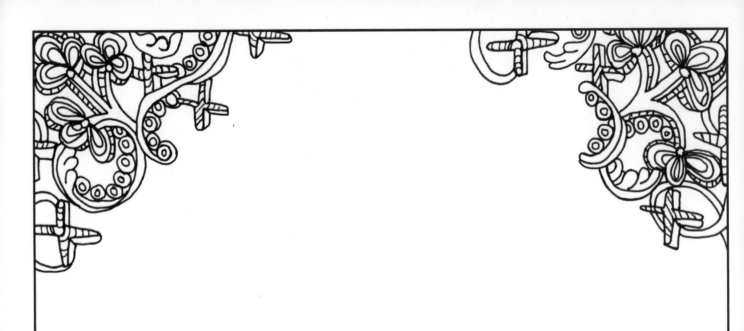

The cat is a dilettante in fur.

—THEOPHILE GAUTIER

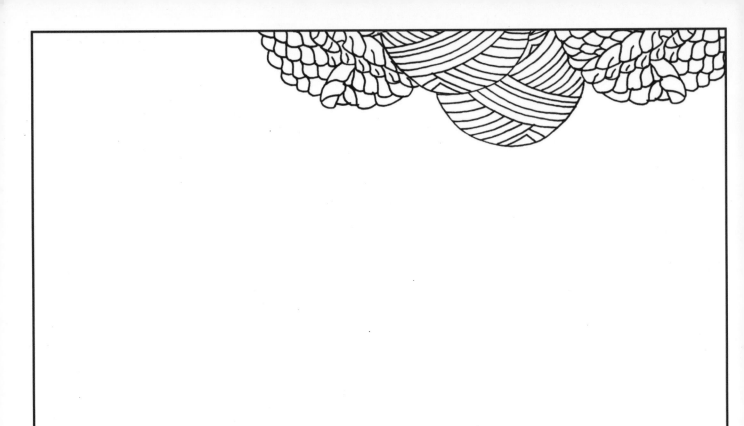

One cat just leads to another.

—ERNEST HEMINGWAY

Cats can work out mathematically the

exact place to sit that will cause

most inconvenience.

—PAM BROWN

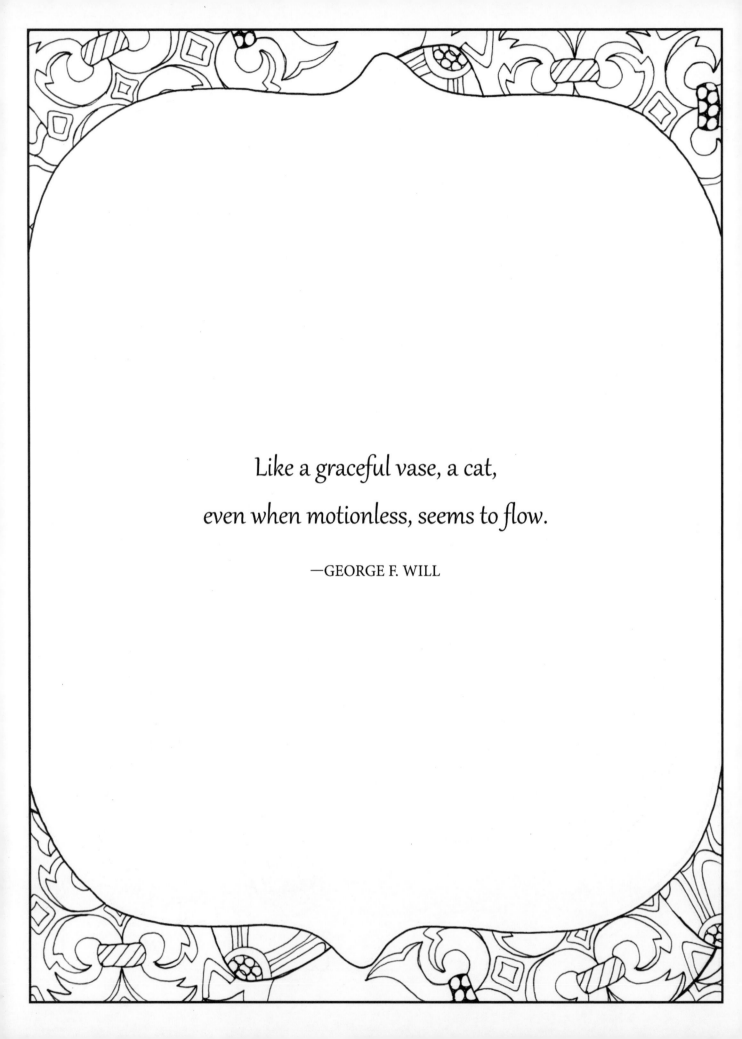

Like a graceful vase, a cat,

even when motionless, seems to flow.

—GEORGE F. WILL

There is no more intrepid explorer

than a kitten.

—JULES CHAMP FLEURY

If there were to be a universal sound depicting peace,

I would surely vote for the purr.

—BARBARA L. DIAMOND

In a cat's eye, all things belong to cats.

—ENGLISH PROVERB

A cat improves the garden wall in sunshine,

and the hearth in foul weather.

—JUDITH MERKLE RILEY

Dogs have owners, cats have staff.

—AUTHOR UNKNOWN

A cat is a lion in a jungle of small bushes.

—INDIAN PROVERB

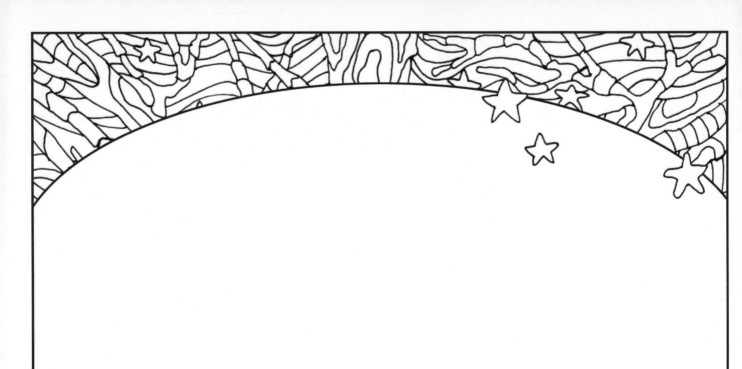

Every dog has his day—

but the nights are reserved for the cats.

—AUTHOR UNKNOWN

"Meow" is like aloha—it can mean anything.

—HANK KETCHUM

Prowling his own quiet backyard

or asleep by the fire, he is still only a

whisker away from the wilds.

—JEAN BURDEN, *CELEBRATION OF CATS*

A kitten is, in the animal world, what a

rosebud is in the garden.

—ROBERT SOUTHEY

I realized that cats make a perfect audience,

they don't laugh at you, they never contradict you,

there's no need to impress them, and

they won't divulge your secrets.

—ELLE NEWMARK, *THE BOOK OF UNHOLY MISCHIEF*

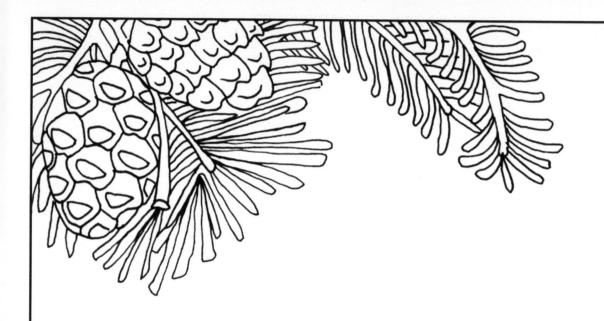

Cats do not have to be shown how to have a good time,

for they are unfailing ingenious in that respect.

—JAMES MASON

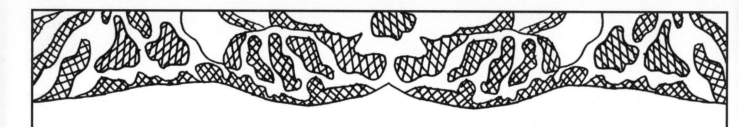

I love cats because I enjoy my home;

and little by little, they become its visible soul.

—JEAN COCTEAU

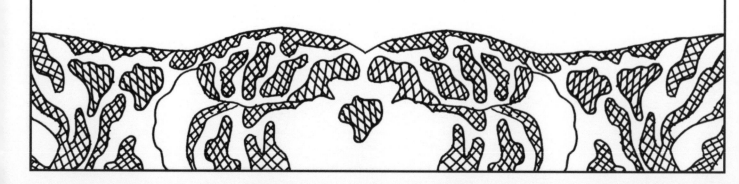

If you like *Inkspirations for Cat Lovers,*
check out our other coloring books:

Inkspirations Animal Kingdom

Inkspirations for Dog Lovers

Inkspirations in the Garden

Inkspirations Christmas Joy

Plus Color-Me Greeting Cards!